# MIND GAMES

## DEFEATING LIES, LIVING IN TRUTH

### 40 DAY DEVOTIONAL FOR TEENS

# INTRODUCTION

Some times life can feel like a mental battlefield.

You wake up with anxiety. You scroll through comparison. You walk around with shame. And in the middle of all that noise, it's easy to wonder, "Why can't I think straight? Why does my mind feel so heavy?"

The truth is, there's a war going on for your mind. It's a spiritual war. It's emotional, and deeply personal. But you're not helpless—and you're definitely not alone.

The Bible says your mind matters. What you think about influences how you live. And even when your thoughts feel out of control, God offers you something better than just "good vibes" or empty affirmations. He offers you transformation.

But it doesn't start with trying harder. It starts with Jesus.

You were made in the image of God, but sin broke the world—and broke how we think, feel, and live. We've all believed lies. We've all carried shame. We've all tried to fix ourselves.
But the good news is this: God didn't leave us stuck. Jesus came to rescue us—not just from sin, but from the mental and emotional chains that come with it.

On the cross, He took our guilt, shame, fear, and failure—and through His resurrection, He offers us a brand new identity, a brand new future, and yes—a renewed mind.

When you put your trust in Jesus, you don't just get a ticket to heaven. You get freedom right now. You are loved, forgiven, and being transformed from the inside out. That's not hype. That's hope.

## How To Use This Devotional:

MIND GAMES is a 40-day journey to help you fight back against the lies in your head and replace them with truth from God's Word. It's not about pretending everything's fine. It's about learning how to think differently—so you can live differently.

Each day will give you:

A Bible verse to lock into truth
A short, honest devotional to break things down
A simple prayer to start the conversation with God
A practical application to move truth into action
A "Dig Deeper" section if you want to explore more in Scripture

Whether this is your first time reading Scripture or you've grown up around church, these pages are here to help you face the lies that hold you back and step into the peace and purpose Jesus offers.

Let's begin the journey—one day, one thought, one truth at a time.

# DAY 1: YOUR THOUGHTS MATTER

"For though we live in the world, we do not wage war as the world does. The weapons we fight with are not the weapons of the world. On the contrary, they have divine power to demolish strongholds... we take captive every thought to make it obedient to Christ."
— 2 Corinthians 10:3-5 (NIV)

Every decision, emotion, and action starts with a thought. What's going on in your mind has a big impact on your life. That's why the Bible says your thoughts matter.

In this verse, Paul talks about strongholds. These are like lies or negative thoughts that get stuck in your mind. Thoughts like:
"I'm not good enough."
"No one really cares."
"God can't use someone like me."
"I have to be perfect"
Those thoughts don't just show up randomly. They are meant to hold you back and mess with your identity. But God doesn't leave you stuck.

His truth is stronger than any lie. You don't have to believe everything that pops into your head. You can take control of your thoughts and check if they line up with what God says.
This is part of following Jesus. We don't let our thoughts run wild. We guard our minds. We take every thought and ask, "Is this true? Is this what God says about me?" Most people don't think that way. But God is calling you to live differently. Your mind is valuable. Protect it.

# DAY 1: YOUR THOUGHTS MATTER

**PRAYER:**
God, thank You for giving me a mind that can think, learn, and grow. I know that sometimes my thoughts go to a dark or negative place. Help me catch those lies and replace them with Your truth. Show me what ideas are holding me back and give me the courage to fight back. I want to think the way You want me to think. In Jesus' name, Amen.

**DIG DEEPER:**
Romans 12:2 – What does it mean to renew your mind?
Proverbs 4:23 – Why should you guard your heart and mind?
Isaiah 26:3 – What promise does God give if we keep our minds focused on Him?

## APPLICATION

Pay attention to your thoughts today. Write down any negative or anxious thoughts that come up.
At the end of the day, look back and ask: Where are these thoughts coming from? Do I notice any patterns? Do these thoughts match what the Bible says?
Awareness is the first step. You can't fix what you don't notice.

## DAY 2: WHO ARE YOU, REALLY?

"But you are a chosen people, a royal priesthood, a holy nation, God's special possession, that you may declare the praises of him who called you out of darkness into his wonderful light."
— 1 Peter 2:9 (NIV

Let's talk about our identity.
Who are you really?
In today's world, there are a million voices trying to tell you who you are. Social media says you're only as important as your likes. School says your value is in your grades or talent. The world says you have to be somebody to matter. It gets exhausting.

But God's voice says something completely different. You are chosen. You are royal. You are unique. You are His.

This verse wasn't written for perfect people. It was written for people who believed in Jesus trying to live out their faith in a tough world. Peter reminds them who they are—not because of what they've done, but because of what Jesus has done.

In Christ, you don't have to earn your identity. It's already been given to you. You're not trying to prove you matter—you already do. You're not trying to be good enough—Jesus already made you new.
Even when you mess up, God doesn't change how He sees you. You're still His. Still loved. Still valuable.

# DAY 2: WHO ARE YOU, REALLY?

**PRAYER:**
Jesus, thank You for giving me a new identity. I don't have to earn it or fake it. When I feel pressure to perform or fit in, remind me that I'm already Yours. Help me stop chasing approval and start living from the truth that I'm chosen and loved. Amen.

**DIG DEEPER:**
- Ephesians 1:3-14 – What does God say about who you are?
- Romans 8:14-17 – What does it mean to be God's child?
- Colossians 3:1-3 – How should knowing your life is hidden in Christ change how you see yourself?

## APPLICATION

Take a few minutes and finish these sentences honestly:
- I feel most valuable when I...
- I feel like a failure when I...
- The part of myself I try hardest to hide is...
- If people really knew me, they would...

Now ask: Are these answers based on what God says—or what the world says?

# DAY 3: STOP THE COMPARISON TRAP

"Each one should test their own actions. Then they can take pride in themselves alone, without comparing themselves to someone else, for each one should carry their own load."
— Galatians 6:4–5 (NIV)

Let's be real—comparing yourself to others is way too easy.
You scroll through Instagram or TikTok and see people with better style, better skills, more friends, and more followers. Suddenly you feel like you're not enough.

But here's the thing—you're not seeing the full story. You're seeing people's highlights, not the behind-the-scenes. And if you keep measuring yourself against someone else's best moments, you'll always feel like you're falling behind.
That's why Paul tells us not to play the comparison game. Instead, focus on your life. Test your actions. Deal with your stuff. Don't worry about what everyone else is doing.

God didn't create you to be a copy of someone else. He gave you your own calling, your own story, your own gifts. And when you stand before Him one day, He's not going to ask why you weren't like someone else. He'll ask what you did with what He gave you. Jesus already measured up for you. You don't need to compete. You can just be faithful.

# DAY 3: STOP THE COMPARISON TRAP

**PRAYER:**
God, help me stop comparing myself to others. I know it's easy to feel like I'm not enough, but You created me with a purpose. Thank You that I don't need to compete to matter. Teach me to stay focused on the life You've called me to live. Amen.

**DIG DEEPER:**
- 1 Samuel 18:6–9 – How did comparison affect Saul?
- 2 Corinthians 10:12 – What does Paul say about comparing ourselves?
- Matthew 25:14–30 – How does Jesus view faithfulness with what we've been given?

## APPLICATION

Try doing these three things this week:
1. Unfollow or mute one account that constantly makes you feel insecure.
2. Limit your scroll time. Set a screen time limit and stick to it.
3. Shift your focus. Every time you feel jealousy or comparison pop up, thank God for three things in your life right now.

Your joy grows when you stop comparing and start being grateful.

# DAY 4: HANDLING ANXIETY

"Do not be anxious about anything, but in every situation, by prayer and petition, with thanksgiving, present your requests to God. And the peace of God, which transcends all understanding, will guard your hearts and your minds in Christ Jesus."
— Philippians 4:6-7 (NIV)

Anxiety hits hard. Your heart races, your stomach tightens, and your thoughts go a hundred miles an hour. You start playing out the worst-case scenarios in your head, and suddenly everything feels like too much.

If you've ever been there—you're not alone. Anxiety is something a lot of people deal with, especially teens. And it's not just in your head. It affects your whole body. You might feel stuck, scared, or just plain exhausted.

Paul tells us not to be anxious—but he's not saying "just get over it." He's giving us a way to handle it. Bring it to God. Talk to Him about what's bothering you. Thank Him for being with you. Ask Him for what you need. And when you do, something powerful happens. God's peace shows up—not fake peace, but real peace that doesn't even make sense sometimes. That peace guards your heart and your mind. Like a bodyguard for your emotions and thoughts.

This doesn't mean anxiety goes away instantly. It means you don't have to face it alone. Jesus is with you in it, and He gives you tools to get through it.

# DAY 4: HANDLING ANXIETY

**PRAYER:**
God, You see what's going on in my heart and mind. Sometimes I feel overwhelmed. Thank You for inviting me to bring my anxiety to You. Help me trust You even when I feel shaky inside. Fill me with Your peace. Guard my heart and mind today. Amen.

**DIG DEEPER:**
- Matthew 6:25-34 – What reasons does Jesus give for not worrying?
- Psalm 56:3 – What does David do when he's afraid?
- Isaiah 41:10 – What promises does God give to those who are anxious?

## APPLICATION

When you feel anxious, try this:
1. Name it. What are you actually worried about? Be specific.
2. Thank God. Before asking Him to fix it, thank Him for something—anything.
3. Ask, then release. Tell God what you need, then release it to Him.

Do this each time anxiety creeps in this week. Even if it doesn't "fix" everything right away, you're building a habit of turning to God—and that matters.

## DAY 5: FACING DEPRESSION

"I waited patiently for the Lord; he turned to me and heard my cry. He lifted me out of the slimy pit, out of the mud and mire; he set my feet on a rock and gave me a firm place to stand. He put a new song in my mouth, a hymn of praise to our God."
– Psalm 40:1-3 (NIV)

Some days just feel tough. You don't want to get out of bed. Things that used to bring you joy feel empty. It's hard to care. And when people ask how you're doing, you either fake a smile or don't know what to say. Depression is real. And it doesn't mean you're weak or broken. It doesn't mean you're a bad Christian or that something's wrong with you.

King David wrote today's verse during a time when he felt like he was drowning emotionally. He talks about being in the "mud and mire"—like he couldn't get free no matter how hard he tried. But he also says something important: God heard him. God lifted him up.
It didn't happen instantly. Sometimes healing takes time. And sometimes it takes help.
If you're feeling depressed, the answer isn't to push it down and pretend it's fine. You can be honest with God. He can handle your questions and your pain. And you can talk to someone about it—someone safe, like a counselor, youth leader, or trusted adult.

Jesus understands sadness. He was called "a man of sorrows." He wept. He suffered. He knows how it feels, and He doesn't leave you in your pain.

# DAY 5: FACING DEPRESSION

**PRAYER:**
God, some days feel dark and heavy. I don't always know what to do with those feelings. Thank You for being close even when I feel far from You. Thank You for hearing my cries and not giving up on me. Help me hold on, even when it's hard. Remind me that You are my Rock when everything else feels shaky. Amen.

**DIG DEEPER:**
- Psalm 88 – What stands out about how honest the writer is with God?
- 1 Kings 19:1–18 – How did God respond when Elijah was depressed?
- Lamentations 3:19–24 – How does hope start to return even in deep sorrow?

## APPLICATION

If you're struggling with depression or just feel "off" lately, try these:
1. Tell someone. Don't keep it inside. Talk to someone safe you trust.
2. Get help. If it's serious, talk to a doctor, counselor, or your parents. You are not weak for needing support.
3. Do one small thing today. Go outside. Listen to a worship song. Write a short prayer. Small steps matter.
4. Stay connected. Don't isolate yourself. Visit friends, church, or youth group.

You're not alone. Jesus is with you, and so are people who care.

# 6: OVERCOMING SHAME

"Therefore, there is now no condemnation for those who are in Christ Jesus."
— Romans 8:1 (NIV)

There's a big difference between guilt and shame.
Guilt says, "I messed up."
Shame says, "I am a mess."

Guilt can lead to change. Shame just keeps you stuck. It makes you want to hide. It whispers, "You'll never be good enough. You'll never be loved if people knew the real you."

If you're in Christ, there is no condemnation. None. God doesn't see you as broken beyond repair. He sees you through Jesus—as loved, forgiven, and whole.

Jesus didn't just die for your sin—He took your shame, too. He was publicly mocked and exposed on the cross so you could be free. You're not defined by your worst moment or your biggest secret. You're defined by God's love.

Shame grows in silence. That's why the Bible encourages confession and honesty. When we bring shame into the light with God—and sometimes with others—it loses its grip.

# 6: OVERCOMING SHAME

**PRAYER:**
Father, I often let shame shape how I see myself. But Your Word says I'm not condemned. Thank You for loving me even when I feel unworthy. Help me bring my struggles into the light and believe what You say about me. Amen.

**DIG DEEPER:**
- Genesis 3:7-10 – What did Adam and Eve do when shame entered the picture?
- Hebrews 12:2 – How did Jesus handle shame on the cross?
- 1 John 1:7-9 – What happens when we confess our sins?

## APPLICATION

1. Write down the shame-based thoughts you've believed (ex: "I'm too messed up").
2. Next to each one, write what God says instead (ex: "I am fully forgiven").
3. Share one of those lies with someone safe—a mentor, leader, or trusted friend.

Shame breaks when it's brought into the light.

# DAY 7: FILTERING YOUR THOUGHTS

"Finally, brothers and sisters, whatever is true, whatever is noble, whatever is right, whatever is pure, whatever is lovely, whatever is admirable—if anything is excellent or praiseworthy—think about such things."
— Philippians 4:8 (NIV)

If someone handed you a cup of dirty water, you wouldn't just drink it. But what about your mind? Every day, your brain takes in thousands of things—videos, music, posts, conversations. Some of it builds you up. Some of it tears you down. What you let in matters, because your thoughts shape your emotions, your choices, and your faith.

Paul gives us a list in this verse to help us filter what we let stick in our heads. It's not about being fake positive. It's about training your mind to recognize what's worth thinking about.

Ask yourself:
 Is it true?
 Is it right?
 Does it help me grow?

Would God want this to be in my thoughts?
This doesn't mean ignoring tough stuff or pretending everything's fine. It means you get to choose what takes up space in your mind—and whether it brings peace or chaos.
Jesus wants you to live in freedom. That includes your thought life.

# DAY 7: FILTERING YOUR THOUGHTS

**PRAYER:**
God, help me be more careful about what I let into my mind. Teach me to think in a way that honors You. When my thoughts spiral, remind me to come back to truth. Help me focus on what's good, not just what's loud. Amen.

**DIG DEEPER:**
- Romans 12:2 – How does renewing your mind change you?
- Psalm 119:11 – What did the psalmist do to guard his thoughts?
- Matthew 6:22-23 – What does Jesus say about what we focus on?

## APPLICATION

Scroll through your social feeds or playlist. Ask: Does this help me think the way God wants me to think?

Make three changes this week—maybe mute one account, delete a playlist, or add a Bible app notification.

Memorize Philippians 4:8 or write it out and post it somewhere. Let it be your mental filter.

# DAY 8: SPIRITUAL WARFARE

"For our struggle is not against flesh and blood, but against the rulers, against the authorities, against the powers of this dark world and against the spiritual forces of evil in the heavenly realms. Therefore put on the full armor of God..."
— Ephesians 6:12-13 (NIV)

Sometimes thoughts hit out of nowhere. Fear, shame, doubt, or temptation can just hit us. Where do those thoughts come from?

The Bible tells us not every battle is physical or emotional. Some are spiritual.
If the enemy can control how you think, it's easier to control how you live.
Satan's biggest weapon is lies. He twists truth, makes you doubt who God is and who you are. That's why Paul says to put on the full armor of God. It's not just a metaphor—it's your defense.

Each part of the armor guards your mind and heart:
- Truth fights lies.
- Righteousness reminds you that you're made right through Jesus.
- Peace keeps you steady.
- Faith blocks fear.
- Salvation gives you confidence that you're secure.
- God's Word is your weapon—don't just read it, use it.

The good news? Jesus already won the war. We don't fight to win—we fight from the victory He already gave us.

# DAY 8: SPIRITUAL WARFARE

**PRAYER:**
Jesus, thank You for giving me what I need to stand strong. Help me recognize the lies I've been believing and replace them with Your truth. Help me suit up each day and remember that the battle belongs to You. Amen.

**DIG DEEPER:**
- John 8:44 – How does Jesus describe Satan?
- James 4:7 – What does it say to do when you face spiritual attacks?
- Ephesians 6:14-17 – What are the pieces of the armor of God?

## APPLICATION

- Identify one lie you've been believing—about yourself, God, or your situation.

- Find a Bible verse that tells the truth to replace it. Write it down and keep it with you.

- Each morning this week, take 30 seconds to pray and mentally "put on" the armor of God. Remind yourself: You're not alone. God's got you covered.

# DAY 9: THE POWER OF WORDS

"The tongue has the power of life and death, and those who love it will eat its fruit."
— Proverbs 18:21 (NIV)

Words can hit harder than a punch.
What someone says—or what you say to yourself—can either build you up or tear you apart. Proverbs says our words carry the power of life or death. That's not just about what we say to others—it includes the stuff we speak over ourselves.

You've probably heard things like:
- "You're so dramatic."
- "You'll never be good at that."
- "Why can't you be more like them?"

Over time, those words stick. And if we're not careful, we start repeating them in our own minds. We need to realize what God says about you matters most. And He says you're loved, chosen, forgiven, and created for a purpose.

If your words don't line up with what God says, it's time to change the script.
Speak life—to yourself and others. Let your words reflect the love and truth of Jesus.

# DAY 9: THE POWER OF WORDS

**PRAYER:**
God, help me be more aware of the words I use—especially toward myself and the people around me. Teach me to speak truth, kindness, and life, not anger or negativity. Let my words match Your heart. Amen.

**DIG DEEPER:**
- James 3:3-10 – What does James say about the tongue?
- Ephesians 4:29 – What should our words do for others?
- Psalm 19:14 – What's David's prayer about his speech?

## APPLICATION

- Write down three lies or negative phrases you've believed about yourself.

- Find a Bible verse that speaks the truth for each one.

- Speak those truths out loud. Do it again tomorrow.

# DAY 10: RENEWING YOUR MIND

"Do not conform to the pattern of this world, but be transformed by the renewing of your mind."
— Romans 12:2 (NIV)

If you want a different kind of life, it starts with a different kind of mind.

The world has a pattern—it tells you to chase success, obsess over appearance, follow your feelings, and live for yourself. But Paul says not to follow that pattern. Instead, let God transform you—starting with how you think.

"Renewing your mind" means letting God clean out the lies and replace them with truth. It's not just about thinking better thoughts—it's about letting God reshape your heart, your identity, and your purpose.

It's a process. You won't change overnight. But each time you choose to focus on truth instead of fear, or hope instead of doubt, you're renewing your mind. And as your thinking changes, so does your life.

# DAY 10: RENEWING YOUR MIND

**PRAYER:**
God, I don't want to follow the same old patterns. I want to be changed from the inside out. Help me think in a way that honors You and brings peace. Teach me to see life through Your truth, not just my feelings or the world's opinions. Amen.

**DIG DEEPER:**
- Colossians 3:2 – Where should we set our minds?
- 2 Corinthians 4:16 – What does God renew daily?
- Philippians 2:5 – What kind of mindset should we have?

## APPLICATION

- Think of one negative mindset you've been stuck in (like fear, comparison, or pride).

- Find a verse that speaks truth over that mindset.

- Each day this week, read that verse and ask God to help rewire your thoughts.

# DAY 11: THE LIES WE BELIEVE

"You are of your father the devil, and you want to carry out your father's desires. He was a murderer from the beginning and does not stand in the truth, because there is no truth in him. When he tells a lie, he speaks from his own nature, because he is a liar and the father of lies." — John 8:44 (CSB)

Not every thought that pops into your head is true. Some are lies—and they sound convincing.

Things like:
- "I'll never be enough."
- "God's tired of me."
- "Nobody cares about what I'm going through."
- "If people really knew me, they'd walk away."

These kinds of thoughts don't come from God. Jesus said the devil is "the father of lies." That's his go-to strategy—get you to believe something false so you'll live like it's true.

If the enemy can't keep you from knowing Jesus, he'll do everything he can to mess with your thoughts—especially about who God is and who you are.

But the good news is this: lies lose their power when you shine truth on them. That's why reading Scripture matters. It's your filter. It shows you what's real and what's not. The more you fill your mind with truth, the easier it is to spot the lies.

# DAY 11: THE LIES WE BELIEVE

**PRAYER:**
Jesus, help me recognize the lies I've believed. I don't want to live stuck in fear, shame, or doubt. Fill my mind with Your truth. Show me who You really are and who You say I am. Amen.

**DIG DEEPER:**
- Genesis 3:1-5 – What lie did the serpent tell Eve?
- 2 Corinthians 10:5 – What should we do with thoughts that go against God's truth?
- Psalm 119:160 – What does this verse say about the truth of God's Word?

## APPLICATION

- Write down one lie you've believed about yourself or God.
- Find a verse that tells the truth about it.
- Read that verse every day this week. Say it out loud if you need to.

Truth doesn't just sound better. It sets you free.

# DAY 12: DOES GOD LOVE ME?

"But God proves his own love for us in that while we were still sinners, Christ died for us."
— Romans 5:8 (CSB)

Let's talk about one of the biggest lies people believe: God doesn't really love me.

Maybe you've messed up and feel too far gone. Maybe your life feels so hard that it's hard to believe a loving God is really there. Or maybe you just don't feel it—so you assume it's not true.

But here's what Scripture says: God didn't wait until you were good enough to love you. He loved you when you were at your worst.

While you were still in your sin, Jesus gave His life for you. That's not casual love. That's all-in, no-matter-what, unstoppable love.

Feelings will shift. Circumstances will change. But God's love stays the same. It's not based on how lovable you feel—it's based on who He is.
So the next time that lie creeps in, remember: the cross already settled that question.

# DAY 12: DOES GOD LOVE ME?

**PRAYER:**
God, I admit there are times I question Your love. Help me believe it's real, even when I don't feel it. Remind me that Your love isn't earned—it's already been proven through Jesus. Thank You for loving me at my worst. Amen.

**DIG DEEPER:**
- 1 John 4:9-10 – How does God show His love for us?
- Ephesians 3:17-19 – How deep and wide is God's love, according to Paul?
- Zephaniah 3:17 – What's God's attitude toward His people?

## APPLICATION

- Write down this truth: God's love for me doesn't change based on how I feel.

- Post it somewhere visible—locker, mirror, or phone background.

- Each time you doubt God's love this week, read Romans 5:8 out loud.

# DAY 13: I CAN'T CHANGE...

"Therefore, if anyone is in Christ, he is a new creation; the old has passed away, and see, the new has come!"
— 2 Corinthians 5:17 (CSB)

Some people get stuck believing, "This is just how I am."

"I've always had a temper."
"I can't stop this habit."
"I'll never be confident."
"I've tried to change, but nothing works."

Those thoughts feel real, especially when you've failed a bunch of times. But just because something's familiar doesn't mean it's your future.

God's Word says you are a new creation in Christ. That doesn't mean you're instantly perfect. It means the old labels, sins, and struggles don't define you anymore.

You're not who you used to be.
And even if the change feels slow, God is still working.
He's not done with you.
The lie says, "You'll always be stuck."
The truth says, "God is making you new."

# DAY 13: I CAN'T CHANGE...

**PRAYER:**
God, thank You for not giving up on me. I know I've made mistakes, but I believe You're changing me. Help me walk in the new life You've given me and not go back to the old one. Amen.

**DIG DEEPER:**
Philippians 1:6 – What promise do we have about God's work in us?

Romans 6:6 – What does Paul say about our "old self"?

Ezekiel 36:26 – What kind of heart does God give us?

## APPLICATION

- Think of one area where you've believed you'll never change.

- Find a verse that speaks truth into that mindset (hint: try the "Dig Deeper" section).

- This week, each time you struggle, remind yourself: I'm not who I used to be. God is changing me.

# DAY 14: I'M ALL ALONE

"Be strong and courageous. Do not be afraid or terrified of them, for the Lord your God goes with you; he will not leave you or abandon you."
— Deuteronomy 31:6 (CSB)

Loneliness hits differently.

You can be surrounded by people and still feel invisible. You might even think, No one really gets me. No one really cares.

That thought is one of the enemy's favorites. If he can convince you that you're alone, he can make you feel hopeless.

But the truth is—you're never alone. God promises again and again in Scripture: I will not leave you. And God doesn't break promises.

Even when people walk out, even when it's quiet, even when you feel overlooked—God is right there. He sees you. He knows your thoughts. And He stays. That doesn't always erase the feeling, but it gives you something solid to stand on. You don't have to feel God's presence to trust that He's there.

# DAY 14: I'M ALL ALONE

**PRAYER:**
Lord, sometimes I feel really alone. Remind me that You're with me, even when I don't feel it. Help me lean into Your presence when my emotions try to pull me away. Thank You for never walking out on me. Amen.

**DIG DEEPER:**
- Psalm 139:7-10 – Can you ever be out of God's reach?
- Matthew 28:20 – What did Jesus say before ascending to heaven?
- Hebrews 13:5 – What's God's promise about leaving or abandoning us?

## APPLICATION

- When you feel lonely, pause and say, "God, I know You're here."

- Play a worship song that reminds you of God's presence.

- Text or talk to someone in your life who points you back to Jesus. You weren't made to go through this alone.

# DAY 15: I HAVE NOTHING TO OFFER

"Now as we have many parts in one body, and all the parts do not have the same function, in the same way we who are many are one body in Christ and individually members of one another."
— Romans 12:4-5 (CSB)

Have you ever felt like you don't bring much to the table?
Like other people have the talent, the looks, the personality—and you're just... there?

That's a lie that keeps a lot of people quiet and stuck. But Scripture makes it clear: if you belong to Jesus, you're part of something bigger, and you're needed.

Not everyone plays the same role, and that's a good thing. Every role matters. You don't have to be the loudest, the most gifted, or the one up front to have value.

In fact, some of the most meaningful impact happens behind the scenes—through encouragement, prayer, kindness, or just showing up when others don't. Your presence and obedience might be exactly what someone else needs today.

God didn't call you to be impressive. He called you to be faithful.

# DAY 15: I HAVE NOTHING TO OFFER

**PRAYER:**
Jesus, help me stop believing the lie that I don't matter. Show me how I fit into what You're doing. Use my life—even the small parts—for Your purpose and glory. Amen.

**DIG DEEPER:**
- 1 Corinthians 12:14-20 - How does Paul explain each part of the body being important?
- Ephesians 2:10 - What kind of work were you created to do?
- 1 Peter 4:10 - What are spiritual gifts for?

## APPLICATION

- Think about one way you serve God and others this week.

- Ask God to show you one person this week who would benefit from your encouragement, help, time, or just presence.

- Don't wait until you feel "ready." Just take the next step and trust God to use it.

# DAY 16: MY PAST DEFINES ME

""Forget the former things; do not dwell on the past. See, I am doing a new thing! Now it springs up; do you not perceive it?"
— Isaiah 43:18-19 (CSB)

Your past may explain you—but it doesn't get to define you.

We've all got moments we wish we could erase. Things we've said. Things we've done. Things that were done to us. And sometimes those moments feel like a label we can't peel off.

But God doesn't cancel you because of your past. He covers you with grace.

He says don't dwell on the past—I'm doing something new. That's not about pretending it didn't happen. It's about believing God can redeem it. The broken parts of your story can become the places where His power shows up the most.

You're not stuck. You're not ruined. You're not disqualified.

In Christ, you're being made new—even if you don't feel it yet.

# DAY 16: MY PAST DEFINES ME

**PRAYER:**
God, thank You for not defining me by my past. Help me stop replaying the moments You've already forgiven. I want to step into the new thing You're doing in my life. Amen.

**DIG DEEPER:**
- 2 Corinthians 5:17 – What happens to anyone in Christ?
- Micah 7:19 – How completely does God forgive us?
- Lamentations 3:22-23 – What never runs out each morning?

## APPLICATION

- Think of one thing from your past you keep carrying.

- Write a simple prayer to release it to God today.

- Remind yourself of Isaiah 43:19 each morning this week: God is doing something new.

# DAY 17: I'LL BE HAPPY WHEN...

"But godliness with contentment is great gain. For we brought nothing into the world, and we can take nothing out."
— 1 Timothy 6:6-7 (CSB)

We all have an "I'll be happy when..." mindset sometimes.

"I'll be happy when I make the team."
"When I get out of this town."
"When I start dating someone."
"When I finally feel confident."

But here's the problem—once you get that thing, there's always another thing. Happiness that depends on your situation will always leave you chasing something else.

The Bible calls us to something deeper than surface-level happiness. It calls us to contentment—a kind of peace that isn't tied to what's happening around us. True contentment comes from knowing Christ, not from getting what you want. It means believing that even right now, with everything imperfect, you still have more than enough because you have Him.

It's not wrong to want good things. But don't let your joy hang on your next accomplishment or answered prayer. Real peace comes from trusting that God is enough—today.

# DAY 17: I'LL BE HAPPY WHEN...

**PRAYER:**
Lord, help me stop chasing the next thing to feel okay. Teach me to find joy and peace in You right now, even when life isn't perfect. I want to grow in contentment and trust You more each day. Amen.

**DIG DEEPER:**
- Philippians 4:11-13 – What did Paul learn about contentment?
- Psalm 16:11 – Where is fullness of joy found?
- Hebrews 13:5 – What does God say about being satisfied?

## APPLICATION

- What's your current "I'll be happy when..." thought?

- Write out 1 Timothy 6:6 and post it where you'll see it this week.

- Each day, name one thing you're thankful for right now. Gratitude kills discontentment.

# DAY 18: FEELINGS ARE ALWAYS RIGHT

"The heart is more deceitful than anything else, and incurable—who can understand it?"
— Jeremiah 17:9 (CSB)

There's a popular message in culture: "Follow your heart."

But let's be honest—your heart doesn't always lead you in the right direction.

One day you feel on top of the world. The next day, you feel like everything's falling apart. Feelings are real, but they're not always reliable.

Jeremiah says our hearts can be deceitful. That doesn't mean your emotions are bad or sinful—but it means they're not the best guide for truth. Emotions are more like signals on a dashboard. They can tell you something's going on, but they shouldn't be driving the car.

The gospel doesn't ignore your feelings—it speaks into them. Jesus felt sadness, anger, joy, and even anxiety. But He didn't let emotions control Him—He trusted His Father's voice above everything else.

So don't ignore your emotions. Pay attention to them. But check them against God's Word. Let truth lead, not just how you feel in the moment.

# DAY 18: FEELINGS ARE ALWAYS RIGHT

**PRAYER:**
God, thank You for creating me with emotions. Help me to feel deeply but not be ruled by what I feel. When my emotions get loud, remind me to listen to Your voice first. I want to live by truth, not just moods. Amen.

**DIG DEEPER:**
- Proverbs 3:5-6 – What does it say about trusting your own understanding?
- Psalm 42:5 – What does the writer say to his own soul?
- Matthew 26:38-39 – How did Jesus handle deep emotion?

## APPLICATION

- Think of a recent strong emotion (anger, fear, sadness).

- Ask: What truth from Scripture speaks into this feeling?

- Keep a note on your phone: "My feelings are real, but God's truth is greater."

# DAY 19: I'M TOO BROKEN TO BE USED

"But he said to me, 'My grace is sufficient for you, for my power is perfected in weakness.' Therefore I will most gladly boast all the more about my weaknesses, so that Christ's power may reside in me."
— 2 Corinthians 12:9 (CSB)

Sometimes we think God only uses the strong, the talented, or the ones with a perfect past.

But throughout the Bible, God used people who were deeply flawed: Moses had anger issues, David messed up big time, Paul had a violent past. What changed them wasn't their strength—it was God's grace.

Paul begged God to take away his weakness, but God didn't. Instead, God said, "My grace is enough." God wasn't looking for perfection—He wanted someone willing to depend on Him.

That means your brokenness doesn't disqualify you. It may actually be the very place God wants to show His strength.

God doesn't need you to be flawless. He needs you to be surrendered.

# DAY 19: I'M TOO BROKEN TO BE USED

**PRAYER:**
Lord, I feel weak sometimes. I feel like I'm not enough. But I believe You can still use me. Help me trust Your strength more than I trust my own. Use my story—even the broken parts—for Your glory. Amen.

**DIG DEEPER:**
- Exodus 4:10-12 – How did Moses respond to his own insecurity?
- 1 Corinthians 1:27-29 – Who does God choose to use?
- Isaiah 61:1-3 – What does God promise to do with brokenness?

## APPLICATION

- Write down one weakness you think disqualifies you.

- Ask: How could God use that to help someone else?

- Don't wait to be perfect. Look for one small way to serve or encourage someone this week—just as you are.

# DAY 20: GOD IS SILENT

"But he said to me, 'My grace is sufficient for you, for my power is perfected in weakness.' Therefore I will most gladly boast all the more about my weaknesses, so that Christ's power may reside in me."
— 2 Corinthians 12:9 (CSB)

There are seasons when it feels like God is just... quiet. You pray and pray, but nothing changes. You read Bible verses, but it all feels like nothing. You show up to church, but you feel distant. You start to wonder, Where is God? Did He forget about me?

You're not the only one who's felt that. The psalmist literally asked, "God, why are You hiding?" Even the most faithful people in Scripture had moments where God felt far away.

But silence doesn't mean absence.
God may be doing more in the silence than you realize. He may be teaching you to trust when you can't feel, to walk by faith, not by sight. Sometimes He's preparing something in you before He reveals something to you.

The cross looked like silence too—until the resurrection came.

So don't give up. Keep talking to God. He hears every word, even when you can't hear Him back. He never leaves us or forsakes us.

# DAY 20: GOD IS SILENT

**PRAYER:**
God, sometimes it feels like You're not listening. Help me keep praying and trusting, even when You feel silent. Teach me to rely on Your promises more than my feelings. I believe You're still with me. Amen.

**DIG DEEPER:**
- Psalm 13:1-6 – How does David deal with God's silence?
- Habakkuk 1:2-5 – What was God doing behind the scenes?
- John 11:1-6 – Why did Jesus delay, even when His friends were hurting?

## APPLICATION

- Write a short, honest prayer to God about something you're waiting on.

- Keep showing up—read, pray, worship—even if it feels dry.

- This week, remind yourself daily: God's silence is not the same as God's absence.

# DAY 21: I DON'T FEEL FORGIVEN

"But if we confess our sins, He is faithful and just to forgive us our sins and to cleanse us from all unrighteousness."
— 1 John 1:9 (CSB)

Sometimes, even when you know you're forgiven, the weight of your past can make you feel like nothing's been wiped clean. You might think, "I'm too messed up to be forgiven," or feel that your mistakes are too big for God's grace.

The truth is, forgiveness isn't based on how we feel—it's based on what Jesus did on the cross. Even when you can't feel the forgiveness, God has already declared you free. His promise in 1 John 1:9 isn't about your emotions; it's about His faithfulness.

God forgives us completely and cleanses us from every sin. That means every time you mess up, you can come to Him, confess, and know that He is there to make you new. You don't have to keep carrying the burden of guilt—even if it feels real.

Remember, forgiveness is not something you earn; it's a gift based on grace. Even when your heart hesitates, you can trust what God's Word says.

# DAY 21: I DON'T FEEL FORGIVEN

**PRAYER:**
Lord, sometimes I struggle to believe that I'm forgiven. Even when I know it in my head, my heart holds on to guilt. Help me trust in Your promise of forgiveness. Cleanse me from every wrong, and let me rest in Your grace. Amen.

**DIG DEEPER:**
- Ephesians 1:7 – How does God demonstrate His forgiveness through Christ?
- Psalm 103:12 – What does this verse say about the extent of God's forgiveness?
- Isaiah 1:18 – How does God invite you to see your sins forgiven completely?

## APPLICATION

- Write down one sin or mistake you keep replaying in your mind.

- Read 1 John 1:9 out loud and remind yourself that God's promise is for you.

- Each day this week, thank God for His complete forgiveness—even when you don't feel it.

# DAY 22: I HAVE TO EARN GOD'S LOVE

"But if we confess our sins, He is faithful and just to forgive us our sins and to cleanse us from all unrighteousness."
— 1 John 1:9 (CSB)

It's easy to fall into the trap of thinking God only loves you when you're doing everything right.

Pray enough, read the Bible enough, serve at church, avoid sin—then maybe, maybe He'll be happy with you.

But that's not the gospel. That's religion based on performance.

Romans 5:8 blows that lie up completely. God didn't wait for you to clean yourself up. He proved His love while you were still a sinner—when you had nothing to offer. That's grace.

You can't earn God's love. You don't have to. He's already poured it out through Jesus.
Yes, your choices matter. But they flow from love, not for love. You obey God because you are loved, not to get loved.

That truth will free you from guilt and drive you toward a deeper relationship with Him—not out of fear, but out of joy.

# DAY 22: I HAVE TO EARN GOD'S LOVE

**PRAYER:**
God, thank You for loving me when I didn't deserve it. I don't want to live like I have to earn Your approval. Help me rest in Your love and respond to it—not work for it. Let my life reflect grace, not pressure. Amen.

**DIG DEEPER:**
- Titus 3:4-5 – What saves us: works or mercy?
- Ephesians 2:8-9 – How is salvation described?
- Galatians 2:21 – What happens if we try to earn what Jesus already gave?

## APPLICATION

- Think of one thing you've been doing more out of pressure than joy.

- Ask: Am I doing this to get love—or because I'm already loved?

- This week, start each day with this truth: God's love for me is not based on my performance.

# DAY 23: THE STRUGGLE WILL NEVER END

"Let us not get tired of doing good, for we will reap at the proper time if we don't give up."
— Galatians 6:9 (CSB)

Some struggles don't go away overnight.
You pray, but the temptation is still there.
You try to change, but fall into the same patterns.
You wonder, "Why is this still a thing in my life?"

When something feels like it's never going to end—anxiety, a hidden sin, a constant battle in your mind—it's easy to feel defeated. You might think, "Maybe this is just who I am now."

But God doesn't see you as a lost cause. He sees someone in process. Someone He's still shaping. And sometimes the process is slow because He's building something stronger than just quick results—He's building endurance, faith, and trust.

Paul says not to give up because you will reap at the right time. God's timing isn't always your timing, but His promises are still true.

Spiritual growth isn't always loud or visible. Some of it happens quietly—when you keep showing up, keep praying, keep fighting, even when it's hard. That's where real transformation takes root.
You're not stuck. You're being refined.

# DAY 23: THE STRUGGLE WILL NEVER END

**PRAYER:**
God, I'm tired. I keep struggling, and sometimes I feel like it'll never get better. But I believe You're still working. Give me the strength to keep showing up, to keep growing, and to keep trusting You even when I don't see change yet. Amen.

**DIG DEEPER:**
- James 1:2-4 – What does God build through perseverance?
- Romans 5:3-5 – How does hope rise from hardship?
- 2 Corinthians 4:16-18 – What does this say about temporary struggles?

## APPLICATION

- Write down one area of your life that feels stuck in a cycle.

- Ask God to help you take one faithful step today—whether it's prayer, accountability, or just not giving in.

- Repeat this truth to yourself this week: "God is working even when I don't see progress."

# DAY 24: WORTH COMES FROM WHAT I DO

"For you are saved by grace through faith, and this is not from yourselves; it is God's gift—not from works, so that no one can boast."
— Ephesians 2:8-9 (CSB)

We live in a performance-driven world.
Get better grades. Make the team. Win followers. Impress people. Achieve more. Then maybe, you'll matter.

That same mindset can sneak into our relationship with God too. We start thinking, If I mess up, He'll stop loving me. If I do more, He'll be proud of me.
But that's not how grace works.

Your worth isn't found in what you do—it's found in what Jesus already did.

Ephesians 2 says you're saved by grace, not works. That means you didn't earn it, and you don't have to hustle to keep it. You don't have to perform to prove your value. God already gave it to you through Christ. That changes everything.

Now, instead of living for approval, you can live from it. You serve because you're loved—not to get love. You obey not to be accepted, but because you already are. When you stop trying to earn worth, you can finally rest in it.

# DAY 24: WORTH COMES FROM WHAT I DO

**PRAYER:**
Jesus, thank You that I don't have to perform to be loved. Help me stop chasing my value in achievements or approval. Teach me to live from Your grace—not for people's applause. Remind me that I'm already enough in You. Amen.

**DIG DEEPER:**
- Galatians 3:3 – What warning does Paul give about relying on works?
- Romans 3:23-24 – What does God freely give us through Jesus?
- Titus 3:4-5 – What actually saves us?

## APPLICATION

- Ask yourself honestly: Where do I find my worth—what I do or who I am in Christ?

- Write out Ephesians 2:8-9 and keep it somewhere visible this week.

- Each time you feel pressure to prove yourself, stop and say: "My identity is a gift, not a goal."

# DAY 25: I CAN DO THIS ON MY OWN

"I am the vine; you are the branches. The one who remains in me and I in him produces much fruit, because you can do nothing without me."
— John 15:5 (CSB)

Sometimes we treat God like Wi-Fi—we only connect when we really need Him.

You get overwhelmed, then you pray. You mess up, then you open your Bible. But most of the time, you're trying to handle life yourself. And maybe deep down, you think: I've got this. I can manage.

But Jesus says something that flips that thinking: "You can do nothing without me."
That's not Him being harsh. It's Him being honest. He's the source, and we're the branches. Without the vine, branches dry up. No growth. No fruit. No strength.

Trying to live your faith without Jesus at the center will leave you burned out, frustrated, or fake. You might still be busy doing "Christian stuff," but your soul will feel empty.

Real spiritual life flows from staying close to Him—not just on Sundays, but every day. That's what it means to remain in Him: stay connected, stay dependent, stay in step with Him.
God doesn't need your independence. He wants your dependence.

# DAY 25: I CAN DO THIS ON MY OWN

**PRAYER:**
Jesus, I admit I try to do life on my own too often. Help me stay connected to You—not just when things fall apart, but every day. Teach me to depend on You for everything. You are the source of everything good in my life. Amen.

**DIG DEEPER:**
- Proverbs 3:5-6 – What happens when we trust God instead of ourselves?
- Psalm 63:1 – What kind of hunger and thirst does David describe?
- Galatians 5:25 – What does it mean to keep in step with the Spirit?

## APPLICATION

- Start each day this week with a simple prayer: "God, I need You today."

- Pay attention to moments when you're relying more on yourself than on Him—and invite Him into them.

- Pick one way to stay connected daily—prayer, a verse, worship music, or journaling—and commit to it this week.

# DAY 26: I'M FALLING BEHIND

"The Lord is not slow in keeping his promise, as some understand slowness, but is patient with you, not wanting any to perish but all to come to repentance."
— 2 Peter 3:9 (CSB)

It's easy to feel like everyone else is ahead of you. They're getting scholarships, relationships, confidence, direction... and you're still figuring things out.

You scroll and compare. You see friends posting about their accomplishments and wonder why your journey looks so different. You wonder, "What's wrong with me? Why am I not there yet?"

But here's the truth: God's not in a rush with you. His timing isn't like yours. While you feel behind, He's working patiently, intentionally, and wisely. What feels slow to you might actually be grace—He's preparing you, protecting you, growing you.

The Bible says God is never late. He's never holding out on you. He's shaping your story at the pace that's best for your heart and future. Think about it - some of your greatest growth happens in these waiting seasons when you learn to trust Him more.

You're not falling behind. You're right where He has you. And when the time is right, He'll move.

# DAY 26: I'M FALLING BEHIND

**PRAYER:**
God, help me stop comparing my life to everyone else's. Remind me that You have a plan for me—and Your timing is better than mine. Help me trust that I'm not behind. I'm in Your hands. Amen.

**DIG DEEPER:**
- Psalm 37:7 - What does it look like to wait patiently on God?
- Isaiah 40:31 - What happens to those who wait on the Lord?
- Habakkuk 2:3 - What does God say about the vision and timing?

## APPLICATION

- Write down one area where you feel "behind."

- Ask: What might God be doing in me while I wait?

- Each time comparison hits this week, say this to yourself: "God's not late—He's just preparing me."

# DAY 27: I CAN'T TRUST ANYONE

"Trust in the Lord with all your heart, and do not rely on your own understanding; in all your ways know him, and he will make your paths straight."
— Proverbs 3:5-6 (CSB)

Maybe you've been hurt by people you trusted—friends who betrayed you, adults who failed you, or leaders who didn't live up to what they said. And now, you find yourself thinking, "I can't trust anyone." That makes sense. When trust gets broken, it creates walls. And over time, those walls can even start to block your trust in God.

But here's the truth: God is not like people. He doesn't fail, lie, or switch up on you. He doesn't forget or flake or fake. He is consistent, faithful, and good—even when others aren't.

Proverbs 3 doesn't say trust people with all your heart. It says trust the Lord. He's the only one who will never let you down.

That doesn't mean trusting people again will be easy—but it starts with learning to trust God first. When your trust is rooted in Him, you can heal and begin to rebuild.

You don't have to do relationships out of fear. God can teach you how to walk with wisdom, forgiveness, and discernment.

# DAY 27: I CAN'T TRUST ANYONE

**PRAYER:**
God, You know the ways I've been hurt and let down. Help me not carry those wounds into how I see You. Teach me to trust You fully, and help me learn how to trust others again—with wisdom and grace. Amen.

**DIG DEEPER:**
- Psalm 118:8-9 – Where is it better to place your trust?
- Isaiah 26:3-4 – What does trusting God produce in us?
- 2 Timothy 2:13 – What happens when people are unfaithful?

## APPLICATION

- Identify one area where trust has been hard—family, friends, leadership, etc.

- Talk to God honestly about it. He can handle your frustration and fear.

- Ask God to help you take one step toward healing trust this week—whether that's a conversation, forgiveness, or simply praying for someone who hurt you.

# DAY 28: IS GOD FAIR?

"For my thoughts are not your thoughts, and your ways are not my ways. This is the Lord's declaration."
— Isaiah 55:8 (CSB)

There are times when life just doesn't seem fair.

You do the right thing, and things still go wrong.

Someone else messes up and gets blessed. You pray, and it feels like silence. You start to wonder, "If God is fair, why is this happening?"

God is is always just, wise, and good. Sometimes it might seem like He's being unfair, but He's not.

What we call "unfair" is often God working in a way we don't understand yet. His view is bigger than ours. Isaiah 55 reminds us: God's ways are not our ways. He sees the whole story when we're just looking at one scene.

And here's the wild thing: if God was strictly fair, we'd all be in trouble. None of us deserve grace—but God gives it anyway. That's not fairness. That's mercy. And that's the heart of the gospel.

So when life feels unfair, trust His character. He's not ignoring you. He's preparing you for the future. He has a plan for your life.

# DAY 28: IS GOD FAIR?

**PRAYER:**
God, sometimes I don't understand why things happen the way they do. Help me trust You when life feels unfair. Remind me that You're not distant or cruel—You're good, even when I don't get it. Teach me to rely on Your wisdom, not my emotions. Amen.

**DIG DEEPER:**
- Psalm 73:2–3, 16–17 – What changed the writer's perspective on fairness?
- Romans 9:14–16 – What does this teach us about God's mercy?
- Job 38:1–4 – How does God respond to Job's questions?

## APPLICATION

- Write down one thing in your life that feels unfair.

- Ask God to help you trust His purpose in it—not just demand answers.

- Each time you feel that frustration rise, say this: "God's ways are higher than mine. I trust His heart, even when I don't get His plan."

# DAY 29: IT'S TOO LATE FOR ME

"Because of the Lord's faithful love we do not perish, for his mercies never end. They are new every morning; great is your faithfulness!"
— Lamentations 3:22-23 (CSB)

Maybe you've messed up more than once. Maybe you've ignored God for a while. Or maybe you feel like you missed your chance to get it right.

You might be thinking, "It's too late for me. God's probably done with me."

But here's the truth: If you're still breathing, God's not finished.

Lamentations reminds us that God's mercies are new every morning. That means every single day is a fresh start. Not because you earned it—but because His love never runs out.

God isn't in the business of giving up on people. Think of Peter—he denied Jesus three times, but Jesus restored him and used him to lead the Church. Your story isn't over because of one chapter.

God knows how to rewrite broken stories. He specializes in comebacks. And no mistake, no season, no silence is too far gone for Him to redeem.
It's not too late for you. It's just not. He is faithful to us, even when we are not faithful.

# DAY 29: IT'S TOO LATE FOR ME

**PRAYER:**
Father, thank You that Your mercy never runs out. Sometimes I feel like I've missed my moment or messed up too much. Remind me that You still have a plan for me, and that You're not finished with my story. Give me the courage to start again. Amen.

**DIG DEEPER:**
- Joel 2:25 – What does God promise to restore?
- John 21:15–17 – How did Jesus give Peter another chance?
- Philippians 1:6 – What is God committed to finishing?

## APPLICATION

- What's one area where you've believed it's "too late"?

- Ask God to help you take just one step forward—today—not perfect, just forward.

- Write out Lamentations 3:22–23 and read it first thing each morning this week.

# DAY 30: I DON'T NEED HELP

"Carry one another's burdens; in this way you will fulfill the law of Christ."
— Galatians 6:2 (CSB)

Asking for help can feel like weakness.

You might think, "I've got this." Or maybe you've been let down before, so now it's just easier to keep it all to yourself.

But the Bible paints a different picture: we were never meant to do life alone. Galatians says we're supposed to carry each other's burdens. Not just your friends'—yours too.

When you isolate, you miss out on what God wants to give you through other people: support, encouragement, wisdom, and love. And you also miss out on being real—where healing starts.

Jesus doesn't expect you to have it all together. That's why He gave us the Church. He calls us to lean on each other because we all need help sometimes.

You're not weak for needing support. You're human. And the strongest thing you can do might just be letting someone in.

# DAY 30: I DON'T NEED HELP

**PRAYER:**
God, I don't always like asking for help. But I know You created me to live in community. Help me be honest about what I'm carrying, and give me the courage to let others walk with me. Teach me to both give and receive support in love. Amen.

**DIG DEEPER:**
- Ecclesiastes 4:9-10 - What happens when we fall and no one's there to help?
- James 5:16 - What can confession and prayer bring?
- Romans 12:5 - What does it mean to belong to one another?

## APPLICATION

- What's one area of life where you've been pretending you're fine?

- Identify one trusted person—a leader, friend, or parent—you can open up to this week.

- Say this to yourself: "I wasn't made to carry this alone."

# DAY 31: SPEAK LIFE

"Let no foul language come from your mouth, but only what is good for building up someone in need, so that it gives grace to those who hear."
– Ephesians 4:29 (CSB)

Your words matter more than you think.

They can build someone up—or tear them apart. They can bring peace—or stir up drama. They can speak truth—or spread lies.

You might think, "It's just a joke," or "They know I didn't mean it like that." But the Bible reminds us—words carry weight. Every time you speak, you're either giving life or draining it.

Ephesians 4:29 challenges us to speak words that give grace. Words that encourage, uplift, and heal. Not fake flattery—but real, God-shaped words that remind people they matter.

And this isn't just about how you talk to others. It includes how you talk to yourself, too. The voice in your head should also line up with God's truth.

Speaking life is a choice. It takes maturity. But it also brings freedom—because when your words reflect Jesus, you start shaping an environment that breathes life into others.

# DAY 31: SPEAK LIFE

**PRAYER:**
God, help me think before I speak. Show me where my words have been careless or unkind, and help me change that. I want my words to sound more like You—truthful, kind, and full of grace. Amen.

**DIG DEEPER:**
- Proverbs 18:21 – What power do your words carry?
- James 3:9-10 – What warning does James give about our speech?
- Colossians 4:6 – How should our conversations be seasoned?

## APPLICATION

- Ask yourself: Are my words building people up—or breaking them down?

- Pick one person this week to speak life over—through a text, a compliment, or a prayer.

- Start your morning with this prayer: "God, help my words bring life today."

# DAY 32: FIX YOUR FOCUS

"Set your minds on things above, not on earthly things."
— Colossians 3:2 (CSB)

What you focus on shapes how you feel, what you believe, and how you live.

And let's be honest—there's a lot fighting for your attention. Social media. Pressure. Grades. Drama. Comparison. Distractions come at you fast, and it's easy to get tunnel vision on whatever feels urgent or overwhelming.

But Colossians 3:2 reminds us to shift our focus—not just upward, but eternally. It's not about ignoring your life here. It's about living it with your eyes locked on something bigger.

When you fix your focus on Jesus, everything else gets put in its right place. Stress shrinks. Identity gets clearer. Purpose starts to show up.

Focusing on the wrong things will drain you. But when your eyes are on Jesus, He re-centers your heart, your mindset, and your priorities. That's how freedom begins—when your eyes move from the chaos to the King.

# DAY 32: FIX YOUR FOCUS

**PRAYER:**
Jesus, I get distracted so easily. Help me fix my focus on You—not just for a moment, but throughout my day. Show me what really matters and help me see life through Your eyes. Amen.

**DIG DEEPER:**
- Hebrews 12:2 – Who should we keep our eyes on, and why?
- Psalm 119:37 – What does the writer ask God to turn his eyes away from?
- Matthew 6:33 – What does Jesus say to seek first?

## APPLICATION

- Take five minutes today with no phone, no music, no distractions—just you and God.

- Ask: What have I been focusing on more than Jesus?

- Pick one truth from Scripture to focus on this week—and come back to it every time your mind starts drifting.

# DAY 33: GRATITUDE

"Give thanks in everything; for this is God's will for you in Christ Jesus."
— 1 Thessalonians 5:18 (CSB)

It's easy to say "thank you" when things are going great. But when life gets frustrating, unfair, or flat-out hard, gratitude doesn't come naturally.

Still, 1 Thessalonians 5:18 says to give thanks in everything—not for everything, but in everything. That's a game-changer.

Gratitude shifts your focus. It doesn't ignore what's hard, but it reminds you of what's still true: God is still good. He's still with you. He's still working.

Practicing gratitude doesn't mean you fake being happy. It means you choose to see life through the lens of what God has already done—and what He's still doing.

And here's the thing: gratitude grows when you practice it. The more you thank God, the more aware you become of His presence and provision in your life. Gratitude doesn't just change your mood. It changes your mindset.

# DAY 33: GRATITUDE

**PRAYER:**
God, I don't always feel grateful. But I want to learn to thank You no matter what's going on. Open my eyes to what You're doing in my life, even in the small things. Teach me to be someone who sees and celebrates Your goodness. Amen.

**DIG DEEPER:**
- Psalm 103:2 – What does the psalmist tell us not to forget?
- Philippians 4:6-7 – How is gratitude connected to peace?
- Colossians 3:15-17 – How often does Paul say to be thankful?

## APPLICATION

- Write down a list of things you're grateful for and keep adding to the list every time you think of something else.

- Each time you're tempted to complain, pause and thank God for something instead.

- Text someone who's impacted your life and tell them thanks—you'll encourage them and grow your own gratitude.

# DAY 34: TRAIN YOUR THOUGHTS

"Set your minds on things above, not on earthly things."
— Colossians 3:2 (CSB)

Your mind doesn't just drift toward peace—it drifts toward whatever you feed it.

That's why Paul tells us to dwell on things above. He's not saying ignore real life or pretend everything's great. He's saying train your mind to focus on what aligns with God's truth—not your fears, not your shame, not the lies the world throws at you.

Just like you train your body through habits, you train your thoughts through what you allow in: what you watch, what you listen to, who you hang around, and even how you talk to yourself.

When your mind constantly circles around negativity, anxiety, or distraction, it impacts how you feel and how you live. But when your thoughts are rooted in truth, your perspective shifts, and peace starts to grow.

This takes practice. But with the Holy Spirit's help, you can start forming a thought life that reflects Christ—not chaos.

# DAY 34: TRAIN YOUR THOUGHTS

**PRAYER:**
Jesus, I want my thoughts to be shaped by Your truth. Help me recognize what doesn't belong in my mind and replace it with what's good and godly. Train me to think in a way that brings peace and points back to You. Amen.

**DIG DEEPER:**
- 2 Corinthians 10:5 – What should we do with thoughts that oppose Christ?
- Romans 12:2 – What happens when our minds are renewed?
- Psalm 119:11 – What helps us guard our hearts and minds?

## APPLICATION

- Audit what's influencing your thoughts—music, social media, people, shows.

- Pick one thing to remove or limit this week—and replace it with something that speaks life.

- Each morning, read Philippians 4:8 and pick one word to focus on (like "pure" or "true") to shape your mindset that day.

# DAY 35: GUARD YOUR HEART

"Guard your heart above all else, for it is the source of life."
— Proverbs 4:23 (CSB)

You don't leave the entrance to where you live wide open all day (I hope)—so why do that with your mind and heart?

Every day, something's trying to get in: comparison, negativity, temptation, insecurity. If you're not watching the gate, those thoughts can move in and shape how you see everything. The things we watch and listen to and read all have influence, so we have to be careful.

Proverbs says to guard your heart—not with fear, but with wisdom. Because what you let in will eventually come out. Your thoughts influence your emotions, your words, your decisions, and your habits.

Guarding your heart isn't about building walls—it's about setting boundaries. Knowing what strengthens you and what slowly tears you down. It's choosing to protect the space where your faith and identity grow.

You don't have to be passive about what influences you. You can decide what gets your attention—and what gets shut out.

# DAY 35: GUARD YOUR HEART

**PRAYER:**
God, help me pay attention to what I'm letting into my heart and mind. Give me wisdom to recognize what's helpful and what's hurting me. Teach me to guard my heart without shutting You or others out. Amen.

**DIG DEEPER:**
- Matthew 6:21 – What does this say about what we value most?
- Philippians 4:7 – What does God's peace guard in us?
- Psalm 101:3 – What kind of mindset does David commit to?

## APPLICATION

- Look at the top 3 things influencing your heart right now—what you watch, listen to, or spend time thinking about.

- Ask: Are these helping me stay focused on Jesus—or slowly pulling me away?

- Make one intentional change this week to guard your heart—whether it's a screen-time limit, a new playlist, or a break from something that's been weighing you down.

# DAY 36: BE STILL

"Be still, and know that I am God, exalted among the nations, exalted on the earth."
— Psalm 46:10 (CSB)

Life moves fast. Notifications. Schedules. Pressure. Noise. And in the middle of it all, your soul starts running at the same speed as your surroundings. But God says, "Be still."

That doesn't just mean sitting still. It means quieting your heart enough to recognize that God is in control and you're not—and that's a good thing.

Psalm 46 is written in the middle of chaos. Nations are raging, mountains are shaking, life is unstable. But the solution isn't panic—it's stillness. Why? Because knowing who God is gives peace, even when the world around you is wild.

Stillness isn't weakness. It's where strength is renewed. It's how you clear space to hear God's voice. It's where anxiety loses its grip and confidence starts to grow.

You don't have to fix everything. You don't have to rush. You just need to make space for the One who holds it all together.

# DAY 36: BE STILL

**PRAYER:**
God, I admit I fill my life with noise and distractions. Help me to slow down and just be still with You. Teach me to rest in Your presence, knowing You're in control even when I'm not. Amen.

**DIG DEEPER:**
- Isaiah 30:15 – Where does strength really come from?
- Mark 1:35 – How did Jesus make time for stillness?
- Exodus 14:14 – What does it say to do when you feel like fighting everything?

## APPLICATION

- Set a 5-minute timer today—no music, no phone, no talking. Just sit with God.

- Breathe slowly and repeat Psalm 46:10 in your head: "Be still and know…"

- Do this once a day this week and journal what starts to shift in your heart.

# DAY 37: TAKE EVERY THOUGHT CAPTIVE

"We demolish arguments and every proud thing that is raised up against the knowledge of God, and we take every thought captive to obey Christ."
— 2 Corinthians 10:5 (CSB)

We know that every thought you think shouldn't be trusted.

Some thoughts are true and helpful. Others are lies—designed to distract, discourage, or destroy. That's why the Bible doesn't just tell us to watch our thoughts, but to take them captive.

In other words, don't let your mind run wild. Don't let thoughts live rent-free in your head just because they're loud or familiar. Jesus calls you to take those thoughts, test them, and line them up with His truth.

This isn't about trying to control every random idea. It's about recognizing when a thought doesn't belong and refusing to let it shape your life.

Just like a soldier arrests an intruder, you have spiritual authority in Christ to say, "That thought isn't welcome here."

It's not easy. It takes practice. But the more you do it, the stronger your mindset becomes—and the freer your heart will feel.

# DAY 37: TAKE EVERY THOUGHT CAPTIVE

**PRAYER:**
God, help me recognize the thoughts that aren't from You. Teach me to pause, test what I'm thinking, and take every thought captive to obey Christ. Let Your truth shape my mind more than fear, lies, or insecurity. Amen.

**DIG DEEPER:**
- Romans 12:2 – What happens when your mind is renewed?
- Ephesians 6:17 – What's our main weapon against lies?
- Psalm 139:23-24 – What does David ask God to search in him?

## APPLICATION

- Write down a negative or recurring thought that's been bothering you.

- Ask: Does this thought line up with Scripture—or does it tear me down?

- Replace it with truth from God's Word and repeat that truth every time the lie comes back.

# DAY 38: THINK ABOUT WHAT'S TRUE

"You will know the truth, and the truth will set you free."
— John 8:32 (CSB)

There's freedom in truth—but only when you really know it.

Not just hear it on Sunday. Not just scroll past it in a verse-of-the-day post. Know it. Own it. Let it shape your thoughts. That's when truth stops being a phrase and starts being your foundation. Sometimes we can have a head knowledge of the truth without truly embracing it.

Jesus didn't say, "You'll feel free when your circumstances change." He said, "The truth will set you free." That means the way out of anxiety, confusion, and chaos starts with what you believe—and what you think about every day.

But freedom doesn't come from any truth. It comes from His truth. That's why the Bible matters. That's why your thought life matters. That's why time with Jesus can't just be an emergency fix.

If you want peace, purpose, and real freedom, it starts by feeding your mind with what God says is true—about Himself, about you, and about the world.

# DAY 38: THINK ABOUT WHAT'S TRUE

**PRAYER:**
Jesus, I want to be set free by Your truth. Help me to recognize the lies that keep me stuck and replace them with what You say. Teach me to fill my mind with what's real, not just what's loud. Amen.

**DIG DEEPER:**
- Psalm 119:105 – How does truth guide us?
- Romans 8:6 – What kind of mindset brings peace?
- 2 Timothy 3:16-17 – What can Scripture equip you to do?

## APPLICATION

- Pick one truth about God (ex: "He's always with me") and write it down.

- Set it as your lock screen, wallpaper, or a sticky note on your mirror.

- Each time your mind starts spiraling this week, stop and say: "I choose to think about what's true."

# DAY 39: PEACE THAT GUARDS YOU

"And the peace of God, which surpasses all understanding, will guard your hearts and minds in Christ Jesus."
— Philippians 4:7 (CSB)

There's peace that comes from things going your way—and then there's peace that makes no sense at all. That's the kind God gives.

Paul wrote this verse from prison, not vacation. His circumstances were stressful and uncomfortable—but somehow, he had peace. That kind of peace doesn't come from trust. It doesn't mean you ignore your problems—it means you put them in God's hands instead of carrying them on your own.

Philippians 4:7 says God's peace actually guards your heart and mind. Picture a security team posted outside your thoughts. Anxiety tries to break in? Peace blocks it. Shame tries to sneak through? Peace says, "Not today."

But here's the key—this peace isn't something you create. It's something you receive. And it only flows through one place: being "in Christ Jesus." You don't earn it. You anchor yourself to Him, and He brings the calm in the storm.

You might not understand how it works—but you'll know when it shows up.

# DAY 39: PEACE THAT GUARDS YOU

**PRAYER:**
God, I need the kind of peace that doesn't depend on what's happening around me. Teach me to bring my anxiety, my fears, and my stress to You. Let Your peace guard my heart and my thoughts. I trust You, even when I don't understand. Amen.

**DIG DEEPER:**
- Isaiah 26:3 – What kind of person experiences perfect peace?
- Colossians 3:15 – What role should peace play in our hearts?
- John 14:27 – How is Jesus' peace different from the world's?

## APPLICATION

- Think about one thing that's been messing with your peace.

- Write it down, then pray and release it to God—literally say, "This isn't mine to carry."

- Each time it tries to sneak back in, read Philippians 4:7 and say out loud: "God's peace is guarding me."

# DAY 40: A NEW MIND, A NEW LIFE

"Do not be conformed to this age, but be transformed by the renewing of your mind, so that you may discern what is the good, pleasing, and perfect will of God."
— Romans 12:2 (CSB)

You've made it to the end of this devotional—but really, this is the beginning of something new.

Romans 12:2 reminds us that transformation doesn't start with what we do—it starts with the mind. It's daily. It's ongoing. It's the process of letting God change the way you think so He can change the way you live.

The world wants to shape your mind with anxiety, fear, comparison, and pressure. But God wants to reshape it with truth, peace, purpose, and identity. You weren't called to live stuck in shame or stuck in your past. You were called to live free. And freedom begins when your thoughts are surrendered to Christ and reshaped by His Word.

This isn't about perfection. It's about direction. You've learned to filter what goes into your mind, take lies captive, dwell on truth, and lean into grace. Now, you get to walk it out—one decision, one thought, one moment at a time.

God isn't just giving you a new mindset. He's leading you into a new life.

# DAY 40: A NEW MIND, A NEW LIFE

**PRAYER:**
Jesus, thank You for walking with me through this journey. Keep renewing my mind and transforming my heart. Don't let me go back to the old patterns. Teach me to live with clarity, peace, and purpose as I follow You day by day. Amen.

**DIG DEEPER:**
- 2 Corinthians 5:17 – What kind of life does being in Christ give you?
- Ephesians 4:22-24 – What does it mean to put on the new self?
- Psalm 51:10 – What kind of heart and spirit does David ask for?

## APPLICATION

- Look back over the last 40 days. What mindset has shifted in you?

- Pick one verse that meant the most and memorize it this week.

- Write a short prayer or journal entry as a way to mark this new beginning—and commit to keep renewing your mind.

# CONCLUSION

If you made it to Day 40—well done. That's not a small thing.

You've shown up. You've wrestled with some tough thoughts. You've brought your struggles to Jesus. And now you've got something that can't be taken from you: truth that sticks.

But let's be real—this isn't the finish line. The thoughts will still come. The lies might try to sneak back in. Life won't suddenly be perfect just because you finished a devotional. But here's what's different now:

You know how to fight back.

You've got the Word of God in your corner. You've got a clearer picture of who you are in Christ. And you've got a God who's not letting go of you—no matter how messy things get.

So when the mind games show up again (and they will), don't forget what you've learned. Go back to Scripture. Talk to God. Call a friend who'll speak truth. And keep taking your thoughts captive—one lie at a time.

Jesus is renewing your mind. Not with hype, but with grace. Not overnight, but every day.

So don't stop here.

Keep growing. Keep trusting. Keep showing up. God's not done with your story—and this isn't just a better mindset. This is a new way to live.